When I Reminisce and Reflect

Alice Okunowo

Published by New Generation Publishing in 2019

Copyright © Alice Okunowo 2019

First Edition

The author asserts the moral right under the Copyright, Designs and Patents Act 1988 to be identified as the author of this work.

All Rights reserved. No part of this publication may be reproduced, stored in a retrieval system or transmitted, in any form or by any means without the prior consent of the author, nor be otherwise circulated in any form of binding or cover other than that which it is published and without a similar condition being imposed on the subsequent purchaser.

ISBN 978-1-78955-886-9

www.newgeneration-publishing.com

New Generation Publishing

Acknowledgements

Thank you to David Walshaw, Harriet Lamb and everybody at New Generation Publishing that has been involved in helping my poetry see the light of day, for all the guidance, advice, and continued support. Without you, this book simply would not exist. I am incredibly grateful to be a part of the NGP family. You guys have truly made my dreams come true!

Contents

Acknowledgments

Her Writing	1
Of The Colour Spectrum	2
Better Days	3
These Core Values	4
Patricia	5
A Bittersweet Taste In The Mouth	6
Loss Of A Loved One	8
One Cold Evening	9
When I Reminisce And Reflect	10
Acceptance	12

Dedication

Her Writing

She writes to block out the pain of reality,
in darkness and on stained pages,
of a past life of difficult times.
Expressing her troubles,
through the art of the written poem.
Full of heartache and honesty,
and eyes that tell more than one tale.
Sweat. Tears. Blood.
Crimson from pouring her heart out onto the paper.

Of The Colour Spectrum

A sadness seemed to sweep over her like a heavy cloud, her demeanour sweet and pure, and her smile was the most beautiful feature.

She turned her head and a rainbow appeared in the sky. The crystalline tears that had fallen like dewdrops on a blade of withering grass gradually slowed.

But once her eyes caught the brilliance of the rainbow, her smile shone more than ever, almost blinding to the naked eye, it was as if she wasn't of this planet.

Like an ethereal cherub with white wings so tender, with the lilting of the wind to rouse her dying heart.

Better Days

Nostalgic and still dreaming.
Silent with tears streaming.
Voices in the head screaming.
Swallow the painful feeling.
Eyes fixed on the ceiling.
Broken and still dealing.
Hurt but ultimately healing.

These Core Values

Advice I give to other people, I wish I could lay on
my own heart and allow myself a fresh start
With confidence at full length
To move from strength to strength
To be more assertive and sure
To love myself even more.
When times are tough,
and the roads unbearably rough
To know that I am worth living
and that alone is praises worth giving
To dance to the beat of my own drum
and replace the feeling of being numb,
For these core values I would like to instill
all in the name of harmony, peace and goodwill.

Patricia

When there is someone you love the most,
With everything within you, with every fibre of your being and they pass away, you lose a part of yourself.
Part of yourself goes with them.

In the deafening silence,
seeing the crescent moon rise once more before my very eyes, I am thinking of you always,
My sweet mother in heaven.

A Bittersweet Taste In The Mouth

On the most special of occasions,
like birthdays and Easter and Mother's Day and Christmas
is where I most ache for my mother's presence the most -
like the rug had been pulled from under me
and I had hit the floor with a bang.

Where I was only just coming into my own,
trying to find my place and sense of belonging
and the one constant in my life was torn away from me so
suddenly and I felt all alone in this world. This world I
grew so bitter and resentful towards for taking her from
me, for robbing me of my time with her,
completely unexpected and out of the blue, everything
became a blur, left with the emptiness that her absence left
behind.

Life has now taught me that you can lose someone at the
blink of an eye. Life is not forever, and time is always
ticking away, for we are not immortal beings.

Losing a parent at a young age has been the most
devastating and painful experiences I have ever felt in my
entire life. I wouldn't wish this on my worst enemy,
but I have to let go. Let go and realize that she would
never want me to go through life with this chip on my
shoulder, and with this pain in my chest.

She would want me to be happy again
this experience has changed me to my very core
changed how I see myself, how I see life, and how I

interact with the surrounding environment. I will carry the weight of this tragedy around with me for the rest of my life, and the lessons I have gained because of it.

Loss of a Loved One

The loss of a loved one, as they are no longer earthbound. You will not drown in seas of sorrow or suffocate in the billows of the thick smoke that is angst.

For there is light, and the pain will pass.

Dwell on the sad moments and your mind will eat you alive. Focus on the happy moments and your mind will be free.

As free as the windblow.

One Cold Evening

I take my small strides under the amber streetlights,
the crunching of autumn leaves below my feet,
the winter chill brushing past my cheeks
and only the humming of cars to ease my wandering mind.

The sky a deep cloudless blue with tinges of lilac
so magnificent and pure.
I inwardly smile as I am humbled
overwhelmed by how nature can be so rich and
enticing, in all its wondrous beauty.

My pensive sadness lingers no more.

When I Reminisce And Reflect

Writing a poem, therapy to my beating heart.
For I am inconsolable and cannot control my
quivering lips. The walls are closing in on me,
drowned in my thoughts and paralysed in fear,
physically drained of energy that is inside me.

The comfort and the warmth of a hug to calm my
trembling body, by my dear stepmother, a woman
who had taken me under her wing with undying
devotion. My heart had shattered for her having to see
me at such a low point, my lungs desperate to catch
every breath.

The pain etched on my father's face, a memory that
has never left my mind, when I was expressed
ideations of taking my own life.

A mind that cries for some quiet,
I am at ease when I rest my head on my pillow,
when there is only the sound of blood pulsating
through my temples and the feeling of gratefulness
in my heart.

For the family.
For the friends.
For the abundance of love that surrounds my soul.

The pressing of my ear to the pillow, the sound of my

heartbeat lulling me to sleep
and I continue to dream of a brighter tomorrow.

Acceptance

Accept the current state of how you feel,
acknowledge the feeling and look for ways to reach out for support.

Someone out there loves you for who you are.

Be gentle with yourself.

People are willing to listen to your story.

You are loved, you mean something to somebody, you belong, and you are strong.

Please remember to breathe and keep your feet on the ground.

Share your struggles.

Spread awareness.

And that is a step forward in the right direction.

Dedication

Whenever the notion of sharing my poetry came up, in my mind, I would always dismiss it because I felt like my poetry wasn't good enough for publishing.

I felt vulnerable and anxious to do so. But over the years, I slowly realised that the idea of having my poetry out there for the world to see is a beautiful thing and a rewarding feeling, and with that, a wave of calm washed over me: because I had completed it, could call it my own and I finally felt brave enough to share aspects of my life. And I think that's the most important part in all of this. Writing poetry based on personal struggles and it being published is indeed a very surreal experience and a lot for my brain to process, but the journey has been nothing short of extraordinary and exciting.

First and foremost, I would like to give praise and thanks to God for giving me life and gifting me with the ability to write. Without Him, none of this would have been possible.

To my dearest father and stepmother (my second Mum), you both have been there for me every step of the way, and have helped me in becoming the best version of myself and a better woman. You have taught me so much and continue to teach me so much every single day: to never give up, to stay strong, to fight for what I want in life, and to never stop believing in myself. I am indebted to you both, because without your unrelenting encouragement and support, I wouldn't have had the confidence to even publish my work. Without the two of you in my life, I don't know what I would've done, despite my life having been filled with its ups and downs, I probably wouldn't have even survived it all and wouldn't be here today. So thank you both from the bottom of my heart and for being my safety net. May God bless you both. I love you to the moon and back.

I dedicate this book to my siblings Belinda, Viv and Emily, and my niece, Aya. I love you all.

A special thanks to my best friend Tiffany Butcher and family, to my closest family friends, Bushra and Amanah Durowoju, Taiwo and Kehinde Olagesin and their family members, you guys are absolutely everything to me and the most hilarious, kindest, caring people I know. All of you have had a massive, positive impact and influence on my life whether you know it or not.

And last but most definitely not least: to my biological mother in heaven, Patricia, of whom this collection is inspired by and dedicated to.

In every accomplishment or milestone I achieve, there are traces of melancholy—and it serves as a reminder that the world has continued spinning without my mother in it. But on the whole, I want to make her proud, and hope that she is smiling down at me from above.

Mum, I love you always. Although you are not here physically, your spirit very much still dwells within me. Thank you for loving me and caring for me unconditionally for the first eleven years of my life. You truly are my guardian angel.

About the Author

Alice Okunowo was born in September of 1996 in South London and spent the first eleven years of her life living with her mother. Growing up, creative writing, specifically poetry, was always a place of solace and an outlet for her, and then even more so when her mother passed away very suddenly in 2008. She then moved in with her father and stepmother to Middlesex at age twelve and to this day, is continuously, incredibly, and unexplainably grateful for them for taking her under their wings and for her stepmother for treating and caring for her as if she were her own and welcoming her with the most open and loving of arms.

Alice felt it was right to not only use her writing to permanently immortalize her mother and dedicate her debut book to her, but also allowing readers into the mind of the author and her battles with mental illness over a period of time. She is also very vocal about her struggles and difficulties with mental health on her social media platforms.

Alice Okunowo is currently studying BA (Hons) English Language and Communication with Creative Writing at the University of Hertfordshire.

Social Media:
Twitter – alice2096x
Instagram - alicescreatives

Lightning Source UK Ltd.
Milton Keynes UK
UKHW040956050220
358204UK00002B/147